First Edition
Library of Congress Catalog Card Number: 94-79915
International Standard Book Number (softcover)  0-9643430-1-0
International Standard Book Number (hardcover) 0-9643430-0-2

Published by **Limelight Press**
298 East Park Avenue
Durango, Colorado 81301
303.259.3234

Proofreading by Brianne Connor

To Catharine, who has kept me "on track" throughout this endeavor with her love,
support, and understanding; and to the memory of pioneer photographer William
Henry Jackson, whose inspiring pictures led me into the world of train photography.

# The Durango & Silverton Narrow Gauge Railroad is regarded as one of the world's

great railroads. Each year it attracts hundreds of thousands of rail devotees from around the world.

Its line was constructed in the late 1880's, during the golden era of American railroading. Powered by one of man's noblest creations, the steam-driven locomotive, *The Silverton* traverses some of the most breathtaking terrain ever covered by rail. A dramatic symbol of the American West, yesterday and today, this railroad is truly *An American Classic*!

# The Photographic Celebration of a
# Uniquely American Railroad

text and photography by Robert T. Royem
edited by Catharine Miller

A production of **Limelight Press**

# An American Classic:

# The Durango & Silverton
# Narrow Gauge Railroad

Photograph taken by William Henry Jackson and printed with the permission of the Denver Public Library, Western History Department.

**William Henry Jackson** is one of the most celebrated photographers of the American West. This dramatic photograph shows a train of the Denver & Rio Grande Railway poised high above the Animas River on track still used today by the Durango & Silverton Narrow Gauge Railroad. Jackson took this photograph in the late summer of 1882, and it is undoubtedly one of his most famous.

The Denver & Rio Grande had just completed the line between Durango and Silverton when this photograph was taken. The area pictured, known as the *High Line,* had required extensive blasting and drilling to create the rocky shelf for the track. The huge amount of demolition had left the area barren of vegetation and with a great deal of rock strewn along the river's course. Compare the picture on the following page (the photograph was taken from approximately the same spot) to see the great change that has occurred—along with a tremendous regeneration of plant life, is a transformed riverbed. Torrents of water from subsequent floodings have dislodged the huge amount of debris deposited along the river bottom. What testimony to the river's power!

Also notable is the different size of the locomotives used in Jackson's day and those employed today by the D&SNG. The locomotives used today were built more than thirty years after this photograph was taken. That they are more powerful than those in use during Jackson's day is evident in the photographs: in the earlier years two locomotives were needed to pull a load that is moved by one today.

Jackson's career as a photographer involved frequent work for the railroads. Newly forming lines such as the Denver & Rio Grande needed promotional shots to encourage potential passengers in the big eastern

markets who were hungry for a glimpse of what this new land offered. The motto of the Denver and Rio Grande Railway was "Scenic Line of the World." To assist their photographer they often provided a special private car that included a darkroom and living space for Jackson and his family, who often accompanied him.

In his early professional life, Jackson worked with a United States survey crew. His majestic scenic photography was largely responsible for the public attention focused on areas such as Yellowstone and Yosemite. In a direct way, Jackson helped encourage public acceptance for what was to become the National Park system. In southwestern Colorado, he was the first photographer to record important archeological sites such as Mesa Verde and Hovenweep–areas he had photographed years before his work for the railroad.

The large-format photographs taken by Jackson are remarkable even by today's standards. The glass plates he used varied in size from six and a half inches by eight and a half inches to an astounding twenty by twenty-four inches. He transported his bulky equipment, along with fragile glass plates and wooden tripod, on pack animals throughout the West. Images were developed in a specially designed tent.

Not long after his work for the railroad here, Jackson left Colorado to pursue business interests in Detroit, Michigan, where he began to explore some early color printing techniques. He spent the last years of his life in New York City. All of his labors must have had a beneficial affect on Jackson, as he lived to be almost one hundred years old (1843-1942).

William Henry Jackson left a valuable legacy for all Americans. His photography covered America from coast to coast– vistas of the pioneer West, small towns and cities, people at work and at play. He left us with over forty thousand images, many of which are preserved by the state of Colorado.

DURANGO, COLO. 1883

This photograph was taken by Jacob A. Boston. While he never gained the commercial success of William Henry Jackson, there was a time when Boston ran galleries in both Durango and Silverton.

Durango has always been a railroad town! The Denver & Rio Grande Railroad Company founded the town of Durango in 1880. The D&RG had sought access to the rich mining area in the San Juan mountains to the north for years. The site of Durango was chosen as a suitable base for their last forty-five mile push into Silverton.

When the D&RG arrived in the Animas Valley, a small settlement already existed in the area, known as Animas City. It lay just to the north and across the river from what is now downtown Durango. Reportedly the Denver & Rio Grande, under the direction of William Jackson Palmer, offered the town fathers of Animas City the opportunity to become the railroad's new hub. The railroad sought acceptable properties–at reasonable cost–for their operation.

Apparently, the Animas City council was a bit too excessive in their terms to the D&RG, and the company opted to buy land to the south and establish their own town. During that era, it was common practice for railroad companies throughout America to build their own new towns. The railroads knew that they would attract any businesses in the area anyway, and would also profit in the sale of land that they owned. This pattern certainly followed here. Merchants moved from Animas City to be nearer the train depot and most new development centered around Durango. From then onward, Animas City never rivaled Durango and was eventually annexed by its larger neighbor. The train never even stopped there!

Construction of the track from Durango to Silverton was completed in an astonishing nine months and five days! Durango quickly became an important regional site, both culturally and economically. The vast mineral deposits near Silverton assured the train's success from the beginning, and construction had begun on the smelter (viewed in the foreground at left) before the track was even finished. Rail and mining officials determined that it would be more efficient to haul ore from the mines in Silverton downhill to Durango than to transport coal in the opposite direction.

Rail construction in the area did not stop with the line to Silverton. When the Denver & Rio Grande chose not to continue constructing a line from Silverton to the nearby mining town of Ouray, the industrious Otto Mears formed the Rio Grande Southern Railroad. The RGS (also a narrow gauge operation) linked the mining communities of Rico, Ophir, and Telluride with the Denver & Rio Grande on both ends. Durango became the heart of America's narrow gauge railroading. Lines connected to Farmington, New Mexico in the south, east to Alamosa and beyond, along with the Silverton Branch and lines throughout the San Juan Mountains.

Will Rogers once said of Durango: "It's out of the way, and darn glad of it." Today, Durango is not as "out of the way" as it once was. Modern transportation and a growing disillusion with urban life in America have turned Durango into a thriving and growing community.

Evidence of the change the area has seen is in the foreground of the picture at right and in the photograph on the previous page. Most noticeable is the absence of the smelter in the more recent photograph, an indication of the mining industry's demise locally. Incidentally, this was the site used to produce the uranium ore for the world's first atomic bomb, manufactured in nearby New Mexico. The radioactive tailings produced here were moved by the U.S. government to a more remote site during the 1980's. The scope of that project is revealed by the lack of mature vegetation in the foreground at right.

Today, the mines that brought the train here originally are gone. As in many areas of the American West, the modern economy relies heavily on tourism. The same mountains along the train's route that earlier provided mineral riches, are today valued for their striking scenic beauty. To the delight of rail fans everywhere, Durango is still a railroad town!

A wintertime view of Durango.

The Strater Hotel was originally constructed in 1882.

*Ring out, oh bells!*
*Let cannons roar*
*In loudest tones of thunder.*
*The iron bars, from shore to shore*
*Are laid, and nations wonder,*
*Thro' deserts vast and forests deep,*
*Thro' mountains grand and hoary,*
*A path is open'd for all time,*
*And we behold the glory.*

— George F. Root
*The Pacific Railroad*

## The Durango & Silverton Narrow Gauge

Railroad runs on a spur of track originally constructed by the Denver & Rio Grande Railway. Crews initiated the final push toward the mineral riches to the north during the fall of 1881. Just twelve years prior, in 1869, the transcontinental rail link had been established in Promontory, Utah–America was physically united! It was an era of boisterous expansion, and a spirit of heady optimism infused the developing nation. The train gave Americans a taste of freedom and mobility that had never been known. As the vehicle for much of the incredible movement that was occurring, the train was helping to shape the destiny and even the spirit of America.

In the second half of the nineteenth century, the railroad opened the vast American West to masses of new immigrants. For the first time, the natural riches of an immense continent were accessible to anyone possessing the ambition and sense of adventure to seek them. This indomitable spirit was certainly present in Colorado! Mining booms had already created legends of communities like Central City, Cripple Creek, and Leadville–all towns located near rail service by 1881. The last great prize awaiting Colorado's railroads lay in the remote southwest part of the state, in the rugged San Juan Mountains.

Under the direction of General William Palmer, the Denver & Rio Grande, founded in 1870, had developed a large narrow gauge network throughout Colorado. Rails headed south from Denver, through Colorado Springs, Pueblo, and Walsenburg. Then branching westward, track led to the now famous railroading towns of Antonito, Colorado and Chama, New Mexico. The push toward Durango culminated with the arrival of construction crews in July 1881. They paused only briefly before beginning the advance to Silverton.

The labor force numbered upwards of five hundred men, consisting of many new immigrants, especially those of Irish and Chinese descent. Like many new arrivals to America, they performed their arduous tasks for little remuneration (daily pay averaged $2.25). The often dangerous work continued through the harsh winter of 1881-82, with some workers living in caves they dug out of the hillside near Rockwood instead of the thin-walled railcars that had been provided. To create a ledge out of the solid granite high above the Animas River required the use of tons of blasting powder. Because of the treacherous terrain, the cost for that portion of track was a staggering one hundred thousand dollars per mile! Construction crews finally reached Silverton in July 1882, completing the span that lay almost five hundred track-miles from Denver.

It was certainly one of the most challenging railroad construction projects ever undertaken (ranking with the Central Pacific Railroad's daunting effort through the Sierra Nevadas). The entire line was designated a National Historic Civil Engineering Landmark in 1968.

The arrival of the railroad into Silverton heralded a period of fabulous prosperity in the region. Freight costs out of Silverton, which had been sixty dollars a ton by pack animals, dropped to around twelve dollars by train. The increased access to the area attracted a great and colorful cast of newcomers to the San Juans. As the mining industry flourished, Silverton's population more than doubled (to two thousand people) in

less than three years.

The era of prosperous mining lasted thirty glorious years. Ore prices were subject to changes in governmental money policies and other cyclical market factors. An extended downturn began around 1912. As mining profits fell, so did freight-hauling revenues for the railroad. In this climate of diminishing profits, the Denver & Rio Grande turned much of its attention toward its more profitable routes. Many of its narrow gauge lines were converted to standard gauge to facilitate commerce with other railroads and to prevent other railroads from competing against the D&RG in Colorado.

By the 1950's, the Denver & Rio Grande Western, as it was then known, actually sought to abandon the Silverton Branch, and much of the remaining narrow gauge system in Colorado! However, like all railroads,

they operated under the auspices of the Interstate Commerce Commission and could not simply drop a line at will, especially when people relied on the train for transportation and food supply. The I.C.C. denied the request to abandon the Silverton Branch. Begrudgingly, the D&RGW continued service in southwestern Colorado.

Attempts to bolster sagging revenues with tourism began for the Denver & Rio Grande Western in the late 1940's. A beautiful glass-topped sightseeing car called the *Silver Vista* was introduced to the narrow gauge lines (sadly the *Silver Vista* saw little service before it was destroyed in a fire). Initially, the tourists were included on *mixed* trains, which included many freight cars. Train buffs everywhere were familiar with the narrow gauge legacy in Colorado, and the early efforts at tourism proved to be successful. Ridership the first year (1947) was a respectable 3,444 passengers.

Still, with a base in Denver and an operation, at this point, riding mostly on standard gauge track, the D&RGW had logistical problems with the Silverton Branch. It was difficult for them to schedule crews and allocate equipment and resources to this rather isolated line. Freight hauling was the primary business, and promotion for tourism never became a priority for the Denver & Rio Grande Western. They continued to look for ways to either abandon or sell the Durango-Silverton line.

Finally, in 1981, they were successful in their efforts to find a buyer. Mr. Charles E. Bradshaw Jr., a businessman and train-buff from Orlando, Florida became the new owner. His commitment to the train was soon evident. Under the Denver & Rio Grande Western, much of the line and equipment fell into disrepair. Today, *The Silverton* proudly reflects its place in railroading history. The high professional standards observed by the D&SNG are obvious in all phases of its operation–from car restorations to line maintenance. These changes have not gone unnoticed; today

approximately 200,000 passengers from around the world board *The Silverton* annually.

In many ways, *The Silverton* is a symbol of trains everywhere. It embodies the essence of the classic steam- powered trains that were so instrumental in the shaping of our nation. It also mirrors many of the changes that have occurred in the American West during its span of existence in southwestern Colorado. The train has successfully changed roles during an economic transition that has seen priority shift from hauling ore to carrying tourists. While it may be nostalgic in its appearance, the train operates in a modern context, reflecting the values and realities of American society today.

The original coal tipple is gone, so a backhoe is used to load the five to six tons of coal that the locomotives will burn in a full day's operation. Visible below are the recently deposited cinders or *clinkers* from 480.

23

"...Always mindful of obstruction,
Do your duty, never fail,
Keep your hand upon the throttle,
And your eyes upon the rail."

*Life is Like a Mountain Railroad*
A traditional American folksong

Bill Huffman, engineer, has worked for the Durango & Silverton Narrow Gauge since 1981, the year it was purchased by Charles Bradshaw Jr. Bill has roots in railroad life: his father was roundhouse foreman for the Denver & Rio Grande Western in Durango, and his brother worked for the D&SNGRR.

*"Railway termini…are our gates to the
glorious and the unknown. Through them we pass out
into adventure and sunshine, to them, alas! we return."*

— E. M. Forster
*Howard's End*

The Durango depot looks much the way it did when originally constructed in 1882. The size of the structure indicates the amount of freight and passenger traffic the Denver & Rio Grande anticipated from the onset. They shared the building with another narrow gauge company, the Rio Grande Southern, until 1951 when that company abandoned its lines.

Artists have always been attracted to trains, particularly trains driven by the steam engine. The train has served as a dramatic and evocative subject for almost every creative medium, from poetry to cinema. Such creations are an important part of our shared American experience.

Increasing its appeal are the human feelings we attach to the train. As the first great transporters of people in America, trains are synonymous with change and movement. Powerful emotions are associated trains: sorrowful departures and joyful arrivals, new sights, romance and adventure.

Trains have influenced a rich legacy of American popular music–from *The Chattanooga Choo-Choo* to Elizabeth Cotten's immortal *Freight Train*. The *clickety-clack* of iron wheels on rail, the mournful whistle, the *chugging* of the locomotive–these well known sounds have inspired whole genres of musical expression.

These smoke-rings were photographed on a misty afternoon in Silverton.

*"There was one day about six years ago that the train actually blew smoke rings. They were about six feet in diameter. It was a cool morning, if I remember right. It was something!"*

—Russell Steele is a painter of considerable talent who loved the train as a subject for his artistic expression. Always with watercolors and easel, he was a familiar sight near the train depot in Durango for many years. He was an extremely congenial and warm-hearted man. Russell moved from the Durango area, and is missed by all who knew him.

Discriminating railfans of all ages are drawn to the magical world of narrow gauge railroading in Durango, where toys reach life-size proportions.

*"...it's the nostalgia...As for the Narrow Gauge, I think its great to keep a train, an old railroad, running for the present generation. Otherwise, they would read about it, but that's different—it has a different meaning after you actually ride it."*

—Joe Mayer, beekeeper and long-time resident of Durango. His son, Paul Mayer, worked for the Denver & Rio Grande Western, and was killed in a train accident in 1958.

*"Hear that lonesome whippoorwill?
He sounds too blue to fly.
The midnight train is whining low,
I'm so lonesome, I could cry."*

—Hank Williams
*I'm So Lonesome, I Could Cry*

*"This house was built in 1894. It was built by a school teacher…At one time, when they were building the railroad, there were forty families in here…"*

—Dorothy F. Lechner moved to Rockwood in 1957 and has many stories and memories of the railroad.

Over the winter of 1881-82, the Denver & Rio Grande based much of their track construction out of Rockwood. The area is located about seventeen miles from Durango, and lies just to the south of the railroad's great construction challenge, known as the *High Line.*

49

*"Trains are wonderful...To travel by train is to see nature
and human beings towns and churches and rivers,
in fact, to see life."*

—Agatha Christie
*An Autobiography*

*Caboose* was a term used in the past to describe the galley or kitchen onboard ships. On trains, the caboose usually has cooking facilities and sleeping bunks for crew members.

While every young child knows that the car at the rear of the train is the caboose, not everyone knows its most important functions. On all freight trains, the crew manning the caboose serves as the eyes for the engineer at the rear of the train. The rear brakeman and conductor watch from the cupola for any problems. By their signals the engineer can determine when the train has cleared a switch or successfully negotiated a curve.

Beautiful rose-colored granite like this, found along the famous *High Line,* was a formidable obstacle to the railroad construction crews.

Narrow gauge track is laid at a width of three feet, whereas standard gauge is separated by four feet, eight and a half inches. *Slim-gauge* was the choice for William Jackson Palmer and the Denver & Rio Grande for several reasons. It was capable of making sharper curves and thus more suited to the mountainous terrain found in much of Colorado. It weighed about thirty pounds a yard, one third less than standard gauge track, so manufacturing costs were lower (today, all of the track has been upgraded to handle the larger, heavier locomotives in use). Other associated costs such as laying and maintaining the track were also lower.

Though the narrow gauge equipment was smaller than standard gauge, it did not lack amenities. Parlor cars, dining cars, and even sleepers were found on the Denver & Rio Grande lines until the years of the Great Depression. The D&SNG has faithfully restored several of the opulent old parlor cars to give passengers a glimpse of the glamorous past.

*"Did you ever see or hear a thing that had such a force?*
*That fire and water could pull just like a horse?*

*It delights in eating hot coal a-burning,*
*And the boiling water in its belly churning.*

*It has a piercing whistle. Strength it is so surprising.*
*The water pours from under; Above the steam is rising."*

The Train
A Jewish folksong

The trainmen who work for *The Silverton* are a mix of seasonal and year-round employees. They choose the work for a variety of reasons: some are motivated by a love for the train, others enjoy working outdoors. The camaraderie they find being a part of a crew is undoubtedly another factor.

While for many the work is a labor of love, the train operates in a very professional manner. Of course, the passengers' safety is always paramount. The D&SNG also takes pride in keeping to their schedule. Their performance is very credible considering their reliance on antique equipment. Much of the crews' expertise involves their ability to diagnose and remedy the minor mechanical problems they inevitably encounter enroute.

Silverton was incorporated in 1876 (the same year Colorado became a state), and still retains much of its gritty authenticity and frontier charm. Nestled into a valley a robust 9,300 feet in elevation, its colorful history is linked to the mineral riches of the surrounding mountains. Until 1991, when the Sunnyside Mine closed, Silverton was an actual mining town.

Mineral deposits were first discovered in the area that was to become Silverton when Charles Baker and his band of prospectors visited before the American Civil War. Returning after the war, they opened the gold-rich Little Giant mine. When news of their discovery spread, the rush to the San Juans was on, even though the land was still part of the Ute Indian domain in Colorado.

During Silverton's early years, Otto Mears, a Russian immigrant, was instrumental in developing toll roads that served the mountainous mining area with pack animals. He later established three narrow gauge railroads in the San Juan mountains—some ran over the same routes as his toll roads! Known as the "Pathfinder of the San Juans" Mears was also a linguist who had learned enough Ute to be chief negotiator when the rich mining land was purchased from the Utes with the Brunot Treaty of 1873.

The train's arrival in 1882 heralded a period of growth that did not wane until the first decade of the twentieth century. Silverton was a classic boomtown of the American West and retains that aura today.

*Reportedly, Silverton received its name when a miner was questioned whether the area had much gold... "No," he replied, "but there's silver by the ton!"*

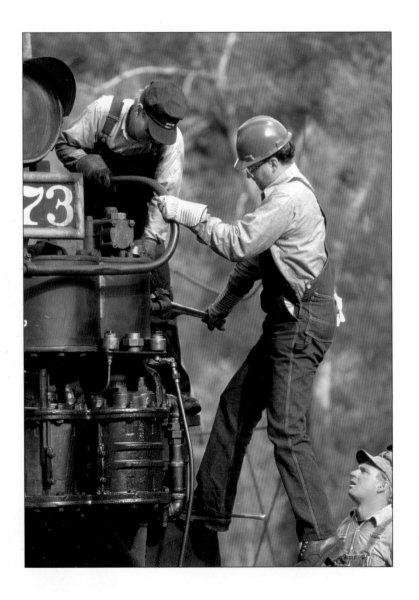

Passenger service isn't the only activity taking place on these tracks. The train is still called upon to haul freight, and willingly obliges. This photograph shows a pickup truck enroute to a mining claim near Elk Park.

Demetrio J. Martinez, section foreman and second generation train-
man, has been working for the railroad since 1957. The term "section" is derived from the term for length, or *section* of rail. Mr.
Martinez and his crew of section men (known as *gandy-dancers* in an
earlier era) diligently perform track maintenance along the forty-five
mile line between Durango and Silverton.

El Rio de las Animas Perditas, meaning literally *"river of lost souls,"* was originally named by Spanish explorers during the late 1600's. The reason for such a portentous name remains unclear. One explanation is that an early band of settlers traveling by wagon train mysteriously disappeared near the river's banks one night. Certainly its waters have claimed many lives. Usually beautiful, cascading waters become raging, muddy torrents during heavy rain or run-off. The Animas, as it is simply called today, can become a deathtrap for the unwary or unlucky.

The Animas is one of the last free-flowing rivers in the entire western United States. With headwaters in 13,000 foot peaks near Silverton, and its confluence with the San Juan River near Farmington, New Mexico, the river drops over 7,500 feet in elevation during its one hundred mile course. For comparison, the Mississippi River experiences a drop of roughly 1,000 feet on its entire transcontinental journey. The Animas is also part of an incredible variety of distinct ecological systems. Its waters originate in snow laden mountain tundra; as it flows in a southerly direction, dropping rapidly in elevation, it passes through pockets of spruce, fir, ponderosa pine, juniper, piñon pine, and cottonwood, eventually flowing through the high arid plateau of New Mexico.

By design, all trains have a link with their natural setting, but few have as striking a connection as *The Silverton.* For most of its forty-five mile course, the train follows the river and its spectacular cut through the mountainous terrain. The engineers for the Denver & Rio Grande decided to build along the river's course, largely, because it was the most direct route between Durango and Silverton. Material shortages during that era sometimes slowed construction crews and often influenced engineering decisions.

Since the arrival of the railroad, the train and the river have had a huge influence on each other, and even their fates have been interrelated. The river contributes to the spectacular landscape through which *The Silverton* travels–scenic beauty that is partly responsible for the train's present day success. Mining activity, conversely, increased greatly with the train's arrival and led to the deterioration of the river's pristine waters.

Raging flood waters have had serious consequences for the railroad. In the relatively short period of time since records have been kept, the Animas has overflowed its banks frequently. There have been three "one hundred year" floods (so-called because they occur, on average, every one hundred years)–in 1911, 1927, and 1970.

The soil cover in the San Juan Mountains is thin, and when rain storms occur there is little to absorb the water. If the rain persists for days, the conditions become critical. It is hard to imagine the power of this river at flood stage. The volume of water entering the Animas, combined with the river's narrow bed creates so great a force that boulders the size of houses are strewn like pebbles along the river's path.

Under normal conditions the river's highest flow occurs during the spring, when warm weather melts the high mountain snows, usually without serious consequences. Average yearly peak water flows are measured in Durango at around 5,000 cubic feet per second. During years of high runoff, the volume reaches 7,000 cubic feet per second or greater, causing some flooding problems in lower lying areas of the Animas valley. The highest flow ever measured locally occurred in October 1911; it was an incredible 25,000 cubic feet per second! The railroad bridge in Durango was partially destroyed and twenty-two miles of track were completely ripped loose and deposited randomly along the river's banks in twisted heaps.

The last major flood occurred in September 1970. Widespread damage to track and roadbed forced *The Silverton* to end its season prematurely. However, the flood turned out to be one of the more fortuitous events in the railroad's history–it caused the Denver & Rio Grande Western to begin an earnest search for a suitable buyer for the Silverton Branch!

My heart is warm with the friends I make,
And better friends I'll not be knowing;
Yet there isn't a train I wouldn't take,
No matter where it's going.

—Edna St. Vincent Millay
*Travel*

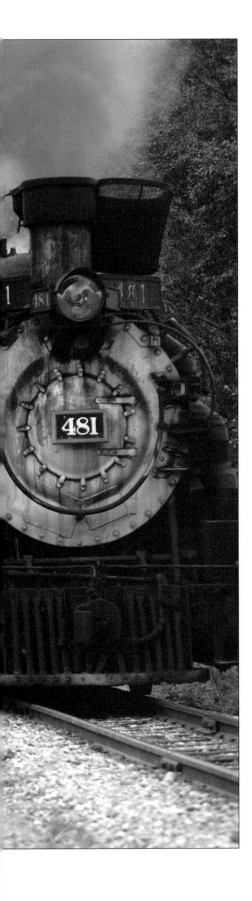

**Elements of nature** are harnessed together to power one of man's greatest inventions of the Machine Age, the steam-powered locomotive. Fueled by black coal extracted from the earth and with water transformed by fire into steam, the massive piece of machinery is surprisingly simple in design. There are few moving parts, and its essential parts are obvious. A raging firebox and the boiler produce the steam. The steam pushes the pistons and connecting rods back and forth, which in turn connect to the driving wheels to produce the movement. The mechanical simplicity belies the mysterious beauty and drama of the steam engine.

St. Nick trades in his sleigh and reindeer for an "iron horse" during the holiday season in Durango! Even the locomotives reflect the festive spirit. Those in use by the D&SNG are adorned with wreaths, while old 315 (which belongs to the Durango Chamber of Commerce) receives some eye-catching lights to help guide its crew of elves. Passengers who ride the winter holiday train are offered one of the great vistas of railroading–from inside a heated car!

**Locomotion** for the railroad is provided today by the hard-working engines of the 470 and 480-Series of locomotives, manufactured between the years of 1923-25.

The Durango & Silverton Narrow Gauge operates three of the smaller 470-Series: 473, 476, and 478. They are from the K-28 Class, built by the American Locomotive Co. in Schenectady, New York. These locomotives actually served the Silverton Branch during the years of Denver & Rio Grande Western operation.

The heavier 480-Series of K-36's (numbered 480,481,482) were built by the famous Baldwin Locomotive Works based in Philadelphia, Pennsylvania. Baldwin was the largest manufacturer of steam locomotives in the world, building over 60,000 engines during their years of operation, which came to a close in 1950. These powerful locomotives were primarily used as freight haulers by the D&RGW before they were acquired by the D&SNG.

The roundhouse pictured here was completed in May 1990 and has approximately one acre under roof. A disastrous fire during the previous year destroyed the original roundhouse, and did great damage to the locomotives.

The turntable pictured here was installed in 1923. It is one of the the oldest narrow gauge turntables in existence.

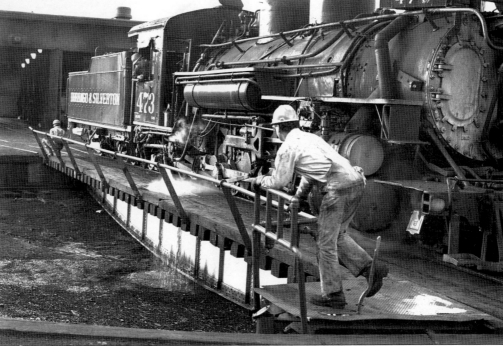

When the creation of this book was proposed, I had more enthusiasm as a photographer than experience. My aspirations overcame any self-doubt–I eagerly (and somewhat naively) jumped at the idea. I was inspired by the compliment, although I was ignorant of the requirements of such a project.

I had begun a professional photography career several years earlier, somewhat out of desperation. Approaching my fortieth birthday, I had spent my life bouncing from one uninspiring job to another. Later I realized I was experiencing what is euphemistically termed a "mid-life crisis." For me it meant changing, quite simply, every area of life.

Many years before I had developed a fascination with photography, but always regarded the idea of attempting it professionally as too impractical. This time, however, was different–there was nothing to lose! The notion of looking back at my life and having not at least *tried* something I loved was too painful. Initially I tried "subsidizing" myself with "real" jobs, attempting photography during my free time. That soon became unsatisfactory; if I was ever to become successful I needed to devote all my energies to photography, and face whatever consequences.

Train photography began for me several years later. I had noticed watercolor artist Russell Steele with his easel and paintings on Main Avenue, half a block from the train station in Durango. I sought his permission to set up a small stand near him, hoping to sell some of my photographic prints. Russell agreed most graciously. I certainly was not a threat to his business; he seemed quite successful selling his beautiful watercolors of the train. The prints I was marketing at the time were scenic shots I had taken in Colorado and some others I had taken traveling abroad. *I did not have a single train picture!*

I pride myself on being a fairly quick learner, especially when the lesson is right in front of my nose! I soon realized that many people came to Durango to ride the train and I had no photos to offer them! I didn't personally know other photographers with a great interest in train photography, so I began to pursue a promising little niche in the local market.

An old friend and kayaking enthusiast, Barry Rhea, suggested the Animas River gorge as a great potential location for shooting the train. He had seen and photographed the train during a recent outing on the "upper" Animas (the portion of the river between Silverton and Rockwood). He related the similarities of the picture he had taken with an old photograph he had seen recently in a book. The photograph he had seen in print was, of course, the same William Henry Jackson shot included near the beginning of this book.

I eagerly set out in search of the spot that Barry had mentioned. Oddly, my directions led me to an area not the site of Jackson's classic photograph, but to an equally picturesque view of the train (it took me two more years to determine where Jackson's shot had been taken). The shot I took there was printed as my first postcard and later, a poster. The reaction to the poster was very favorable, and led to a suggestion by Joe Puliti, then head of concessions for the railroad, that I do a "coffee-table" book on the train!

This is all true. The sequence of events that led to the creation of this book had nothing to do with any carefully conceived ideas of mine. Since the decision to follow my own goals, other people have filled my needs, whether that be in the form of affirmations, suggestions, or needed lessons–even painful ones. I have merely worked hard to develop my innate abilities and remain grateful to photography for giving me a way to communicate. I never returned to the Main

Avenue sidewalk next to Russell Steele, and now, sadly, he no longer works there. I sometimes imagine myself there on the street, and suppose I would do well now—I certainly have a great inventory of train pictures!

What began as a wonderful career opportunity transformed in a short time into a much deeper appreciation of the train here and the wonderful history of narrow gauge railroading in Colorado. Much of the work of the railroad is conducted far from the sight of the average passenger and is more involved that I ever imagined. This wonderful old train runs reliably and safely due to the combined efforts of many concerned people.

The photography of trains has its own unique rewards and challenges, and I certainly learned a lot about both during the two year course of this project. I trekked many miles searching for promising locations to photograph the train. Many of the pictures in this book depict the train, not as a separate entity, but as *a part of* a larger environment. This reflects my personal philosophy concerning the inter-relationship trains have with people and the earth.

Trains follow their own schedule, usually written out a year or so in advance by the train company. That is the predictable part of train photography–knowing *when* the train will appear. The unknowns are weather and lighting conditions that will coincide with the train's arrival at your carefully pre-determined spot. In train photography you may not have a second chance! Choosing film is one area where the photographer can improve the odds for a good shot. Until recently, I never considered using anything other than slide film and still favor the beautiful "chromes" when lighting is predictable, or when the subject will wait until lighting is optimum. When shooting a moving subject like the train in the rapidly changing light of the Rocky Mountains, however, I found the percentage of successful shots increasing when using print film. It has more tolerance for exposure and captures shadow area (especially noticeable on locomotives) better than slide film. Its major drawback seems to be a lack of acceptance by editors who predominantly favor slide film, though that attitude may be changing. Print film reproduces beautifully when it is used in the printing process.

During the two years I worked on this book, my own standards and photographic *vision* changed. My equipment underwent an evolution as well. At the start of the project I used a fine 35mm system. I found, however, that the detail I sought to capture (especially when the train was a part of a larger composition) could only be recorded with a "medium format" system. Such cameras produce a negative three or four times as large as a 35mm camera. What worked best for me, doing most of my work in the field, were the two medium format systems offered by Pentax, their 6x7 and 6x4.5cm cameras. My whole approach to photography changed: I began to deliberate each frame of film in a way that I never had with the 35mm systems and, in the process, recognized elements of composition that I previously missed.

The most important component of photography is, of course, operating behind the camera. I feel that the most beautiful photographs occur in an instant of synchronicity, when different factors–lighting, composition, subject–all seem to meet simultaneously, often unexpectedly. A photographer *feels* those moments, looking through the camera's viewfinder, and just knows that the picture will be a winner. That feeling occurred for me many times during the course of this project. It is my hope that you can sense those moments as you look through this book.